Slo-Mo Tsunami

Slo-Mo Tsunami
and Other Poems

Bruce Dawe

PUNCHER & WATTMANN

First published in 2011

Published by Puncher and Wattmann
PO Box 441
Glebe NSW 2037

http://www.puncherandwattmann.com

puncherandwattmann@bigpond.com

National Library of Australia
Cataloguing-in-Publication entry:

Dawe, Bruce

Slo-Mo Tsunami
ISBN   9781921450433
I. Title.

A821.3

Cover design by Matthew Holt

Printed by McPhersons Printing Group

This project has been assisted by the Australian Government through the Australia Council, its arts funding and advisory body.

Australian Government

Australia Council
for the Arts

for Liz

with love

Acknowledgements

A number of these poems first appeared in the following publications:

AD 2000, The Age, Australian Literary Review, Blast, Courier-Mail, Griffith Review, Idiom, Island, Madonna, meanjin, The Mozzie, Quadrant, Quarterly Voice, Southerly, Westerly.

My deep appreciation to Martin Duwell and to Ken Goodwin for their invaluable advice on the selection of poems for this volume.

Contents

White-water Rafting and Palliative Care

for my late wife, Gloria

If I had understood (when down the river
you and I went swirling in that boat)
that there were those who knew the ways of water
and how to use the oars to keep afloat
– I might have been less deafened by the worry,
less stunned by thoughts of what lay up ahead
(the rocks, the darkness threatening capsize daily),
if I had only realized instead
that help was all around me for the asking
– I never asked, and therefore never knew
that such additional comfort could have helped me
in turn to be more help in comforting you.

I'd have found it easier then to simply hold you
instead of bobbing to and fro so much,
for it was *you* who seemed to be more tranquil
– and *I* whom death was reaching out to touch.

If only I had had sufficient knowledge
in that white-water rafting I'd have learned
that there were those around us (with life-jackets)
to whom I might have, in that turmoil, turned.

Instead, because I had not thought of rivers,
or rocks, or rapids, and gave way to fears
that seeking help might make a man less manly
and liable to betray himself with tears,
I was less useful then, as twilight deepened,
than I might well have been, had I but known:
palliative caring's there to guide us
however wild the waves that roll around us
– no-one needs to live *(or die)* alone...

What to do Next...

after the death of my first wife, Gloria

To lock the front door for the last time, to walk
down the front steps to the path, to open the gate and close it (softly),
to go away as if leaving a dream with the gentle entrance
of morning light
like a family servant,
to travel south as once you travelled north
in a silent epic screening for you only,
to enter a future that has never heard of you and doesn't really care
from a past too well-known to be lived in forever,
to do a polite impersonal violence to your context,
to convert sub-text into text,
to step into new shops as if into Brobdingnag,
to try your rusty dialect and your curious face on neighbours
        for whom you have suddenly just sprouted
                        like a weed from Mars,
to travel on buses and trains and trams with all the apprehension
        of the first Comanche gripping a Spanish horse
                        between his knees,
to leave present friends fluttering like confetti at a wedding and wave
        a sadly inadequate goodbye to such goodness and kindness
                        blurring in your rear-vision mirror,
to listen in the long night-hours to new meanings rising in the dark
        like mists whose dew will record your footsteps
                        in the morning
— to draw up a new blueprint in the hope that it may one day
        salvage from the broken bricks, the fallen masonry,
                the charred timbers
sufficient worthwhile materials to make a home,

to swing around just about *now*
                        and start walking...

On Acquiring a New (Large) Adler Typewriter

Adlerian psychology: A psychological school or doctrine
which holds that behaviour arises in subconscious efforts
to compensate for inferiority or deficiency and that
neurosis results from overcompensation.

for Brunhilde, with thanks

This massive beast now crouches on my table
– gunmetal-grey and, unlike my Olivetti,
asserting such a presence I'm unable
to see how I can possibly, with spaghetti
-like trembling fingers, ever hope
to dominate its Austrian W*eltanschung*
or by subconscious subterfuges cope
with what would trouble a much Jung
-ian person too… Oh sure, of course I set
that quick brown fox once more to jumping over
the immemorially lazy dog, and yet,
in the very process my subconscious ran for cover
and all that I can do now is but wait
for that *under*dog to *over*compensate!

Portraits of a Friend

for Linda

I

I see you always tucking your blonde hair back neatly behind your ears
and those silver ear-drops which resemble tears;
you speak often in soft rushes of words
which remind me of the flight of birds
diving between trees as between lines
of a musical score; a gesture of your long slim fingers refines
your thoughts as though they were pleats
in a garment; your large brown eyes see through the deceits
of this world; your grin is forever boyish and
accompanied by an abashed motion of the hand;
there is also that full smile which can retrieve a
glum occasion transforming the lucky receiver...

The first time I saw you I remember thinking:
here is an interesting person, an exceptional creature, drinking
from the crowded jungle-pool of learning
— alive, high-cheekboned, your being burning
for more than other creatures at the water's-edge thronging.
And lean, lean with longing.

II

When someone enters your life
the door-bell delivers a tingling new sensation,
the phone crouches like a small hairless creature
          which, taken up, may purr with electronic delight
– curious, too, is the way flowers now lean
conspiratorially towards you, their petals spread like a full
hand
in a poker game to which you have just been invited,
gifts pretty themselves up, eager to be the one this time;
meetings outreach the calendar and the clock's
                                        spider-like hands
are no longer crawling inexorably towards zero
but have become slim possible indices of enchantment
– poems put aside their *angst*, rise from their lumpy bolsters
          where they have been lying down waiting
                  the temporarily calming
                              prescription of the page:
instead they now cancel their standing appointments
                  with analyst and counsellor,
find time to stroke the velvet ears of the dog, and rejoice again
in the superciliousness of family cats...

When someone enters your life
the narrow doorway of the day
opens suddenly onto a wide valley
along whose length, beyond your present imagining,
into the illimitable distance there stretches
a river flowing with sunlight and sweet reaches of shadow...

Expectation Valley

As you rein in your bronc on the high ridge
overlooking Hadleyville or Pobrecito or Wrangler
it is coming on dusk or it's already early night
and your eyes squint shrewdly as you take in the scene;
it's been a long ride from Wherever and you wonder briefly
what this miserable apology for a cow-town holds
for a weary suntanned reader who figgers that down there
in a saloon called *Last Chance* or *Lucky Strike*
another dance-hall gal is being brutally manhandled
by some drunken ranch-hand or deputy sheriff
and as you ride in slowly you ease your six-gun-smooth
sensibility in its hog-legged holster thinking to yourself
Just once I'd like to get to page 15 without any of these
doggone heroics and the smell of bar-room powder-smoke
but you guess that ain't on the cards so instead of riding
right on you push through those bat-wing doors
and the saloon goes awful quiet all of a sudden
(as it generally does when Fate, that pernickety little lady,
plays her hand) and your one consolation is knowing
that while Boot Hill is about to be a mite busier for a while
and the town preacher will be exhuming a few old clichés
at least there'll be a persecuted small-rancher's daughter
nestling in your arms by page 186...

Drop-Zone Reconsidered

for Liz

Because I couldn't help myself to begin with
through no fault of my own I guess I fell
and it was a slow falling (since I'd known you
for years before it happened), not pell-mell...
But once I was quite free to have such feelings
I jumped (remember?) as from some high plane
and for a while I thought my 'chute was tangled
but (glory be!) it righted itself again
and so, since you have joined me, we're both floating
through cloud-wrack and through sunlit atmosphere
and I wouldn't know what it was like if ever
our double harness broke and left us here
swinging earthwards, pendulum-like, longing
to be together once again on high
with landscape to be shared below, while round us
were breezes, birds... And ever so much sky.

Poem Beginning with a Line from Robert Mezey

'My Christian and enduring wife'
rises repeatedly to life,
cooks and caresses, folds and sews
as every day she comes and goes
about her works, prays for the dead
(with praises for the living said)
she is as resolute as a rock
withstanding every new wave's shock.

The phone rings, and she's on her way
to revivify somebody's day
– she does not, like so many of us,
count good deeds on an abacus,
her life like washing on a line
where necessary garments flap and twine,
but where all bed-spreads, clothes, and sheets
are hidden from the public streets.

Even so, from time to time, the while,
in an unseen sun, her loving smile
proclaims how someone here can be
close to Our Lord in Galilee...

Old Full-backs

Where do the old full-backs go
when their season's over at last and only the groundsman
wanders out onto the ground to the tiny cheering
of earthworms?

Who rubs them down finally, the staunch defenders,
anointing the stiff limbs
with Penetrene, telling them over and over
they were the hope of the side, the rock against which
the enemy s hopes were dashed?

To what trim-haired up-and-comers
do they hand on (if ever) the fleshly
guernsey they always wore sleeveless, with,
sewn on the back, the two holy numerals?

Is it true that many are found
– fat, gelded by time and a profitable
season or two of up-country coaching
– behind the bar of a pub in an excellent location?

Or do they return as they came, the full-backs, the ruck-men,
grey hair going dark, hands reaching up out of memory
to pull down the mark, the same knowledgeable crowd giving tongue?
Then running the length of the field with no-one to stop them,
everything as it was, only better, the sinews
singing like wires and the air flowing over them
and the shadows stopped dead in their tracks
– until such time as pure myth like a friend towards whom
all of their days they were travelling
takes them in and they re-read the Braille
their imperishable boot-studs imprinted
a lifetime before on the face of the six o'clock news?

Questions of Security at an Australian Airport

Don't know about all this security business...
Take airports, for example.
Went to one the other day
expecting the usual stuff: metal-detectors going off,
solemn guy stepping forward to motion me aside,
explanation (with gestures) to indicate
triple-bypass staples (pretty normal these days)
two hip transplants (offer to show scars)
patting down (deft, gentle, *respectful*),
then request to take off joggers or whatever footwear
– and then away you go, feeling
purified in a way, reassured
another country in the very best of hands...
But last time it was a different airline
(no name, no pack-drill, but it's a synonym
for an innocent person) and I went through
without raising any alarm at all,
so... none of the above!
                               You can imagine
how I felt: disappointed: why, I might have been
a terrorist (an elderly one, anyway...).
But I just couldn't let it stop there,
discussed the situation (*sotto voce*) with the missus
who started to move away from me a bit
then went up to the attractive little blonde
on the arrivals desk and explained my worry;
her heavy make-up could have somewhat masked
her real reaction, but she assured me quietly
that airport security was handled by a private firm
and urged me to approach them and express my concern...
Which I then did, and this meant going downstairs
and going through the metal-detector again
– this time the alarm went off – being a little deaf

I didn't actually *hear* it, but there was still
no follow-up procedure (none at all!),
no being taken aside, patted down, which
between you and me
I always rather liked,
no taking off footwear to put through the scanner…
It was like I didn't really exist in the full sense at all,
and I could feel a ghostliness creeping over me then
so that I haven't felt the same about airports ever since.
When I discussed with my wife the possibility
of going through it a third time,
she didn't agree at all (she had accompanied me
the second time around); she also pointed out to me
in very measured tones that if I insisted
she'd leave me at the airport and since I had no ID,
and no driver's licence
no money and no credit cards
I might have a hard time ever getting out (or home)…

But I still keep asking myself this question:
was I being foolish, or just an extraordinarily responsible
citizen? What do *you* think?

The 'True' Meaning of Christmas

'Aren't we forgetting the true meaning of Christmas
– the birth of Baby Santa?'

Bart Simpson

In an igloo nice and warm
Secure from every Arctic storm
You'll find him whom you eagerly seek
And worship one December week
– That babe (by everyone adored)
Whom half of us cannot afford...

There he lies all cute and chubby
With Mother Christmas and her hubby
Both standing by and looking proud,
Surrounded by a haggard crowd
Of shoppers mostly off their trolley
From trekking through the halls of holly,
Then finding, 'mid the traffic's din,
They've hiked the rents up at the inn.

So, Melchior, Gaspar, Balthasar
If your present gifts should seem bizarre,
Though bought at even greater expense
Than gold, and myrrh, and frankincense
– Remember, our seasons of goodwill
Are meant to register at the 'till',
And that's the price that must be paid
For every Christmas accolade.

But now the Price-Child has been born
Many await that later morn
When at the re-opening of each shop
Parents queue up again to swap
Dud batteries for ones that work
(Who said that Santa is a 'birk'!?)
– While elsewhere Japhet, Ham, and Shem
Rush bargain-sales in Bethlehem!

Good Intentions

for Barney Cooney

Anyway, when Mr Brown came into your mum's small shop
for his bottle of milk this day, your mum said to him,
'Mr Brown, there's something I've always been meaning
to ask you: why didn't you ever get married? you're
such a good man, so I've always wondered...!'
Mr Brown smiled and said, 'Well, Mrs Cooney, I'll tell you.
You see, when I was seventeen, eighteen
of course I'd thought about girls, but I knew my Mum
wasn't going to last much longer, so I thought
I'd look after her first, and then, when she'd gone,
I'd get myself a girl. And the day she died
she grabbed my arm and said, *Son, I want you to go out now
and find yourself a nice young girl.*
And, Mrs Cooney, I was forty-five.'

Preferred Option

Given a choice
I would walk forever in the cool morning
before sunrise when there is no moon
to resurrect shadows and mime the sun
and there'd be a soft breeze like prayer
coming off the rippled water
and the cannonade of distant surf
surging on the far side of Bribie
while my dog would be nosing her independent way
through her earth-bound world happily indifferent
to the far stars as she quests for yesterday's
elusive memories and the messages
temporarily lost

Alive in that darkness there'd be
an anodyne to all pain and suffering
with just the two of us and the sky so deep
that the pale prose of day
with its imperatives and necessary forms
would completely be forgotten...

Sacrifices

I think of the nameless sparrows and the doves,
goats, calves, and lambs, the firstlings of the flock,
and though I'm tribal too I loathe the loves
that justify such slaughterings and mock
the living loving God to whom we turn
desperate for Him to reveal to us
His mercy, while the altar fires burn
and the choicest bits feed priests made ravenous...

Some time in the future there may be
a passover when our thanks for what it meant
will not demand such blesséd savagery
and the tabernacle be a wholesome tent
where birds and beasts and humankind will live
together in a peace not bought with blood
and life will be a treasured thing we give
to all that's risen from primeval mud.

Slow-Mo Tsunami

a Sunshine Coast perspective

Beyond us, spindly-limbed, the paper-barks
are crowding together in detention-centres...
Creeks vanish. Dingy sculpted waterways
plead astronomical prices.
Land-sales offices appear... On bulldozed land
magpies scrounge and plovers in their stillness
listen intently to the cryptic sounds of progress.

Dunny Doos and Portaloos lugubriously announce
carpenters' and brickies' advent.
Skips, chocka with off-cuts, replace Skippy,
and even the cane-toads, once cruciform on roadways,
have long since headed out for Kakadu.
Soon the first 'homes' appear: rendered-concrete
behemoths whose sharp-angled impersonality
poses the question: what but well-honed
neighbourlessness could live here?
Estate agents' hoardings everywhere invite
weekend inspections between 1 and 2,
automatic sprinklers husbanding green lawns
while the lyricism of the pastoral world is plundered
for terms to match the Dreaming up ahead.
Like some slo-mo tsunami, the 'big drift'
is swallowing the north-eastern seaboard;
the thirst of property-developers still unquenched,
the present lamentation of local dignitaries
over the destruction of 'the natural charm'
of their respective localities is as poignant
as Hereward's last stand on the island of Ely,
or that of Crazy Horse on the Little Bighorn...

Incidentals

In a film clip of a massacre in the Balkans
in the 1990s, all the victims-to-be are lying
face-down and motionless, waiting...
                              Except for
one young man who changes the position of his feet,
in order it seems, to be more comfortable.
This penultimate physical movement
has remained with me for years, appalling in its
incidental human-ness, like those shots
of rolled up fore-arms of the dead in any conflict,
the tidyness that illuminates the waste,
the sense of order in the midst of vile disorder,
the readiness for life still signified
the touching hope disabused by the dark angel,
the sense we continue to have
that this day, this hour, this moment
is not necessarily our last.

Why Liberation From Dictatorship May Take Some Time...

Our Great and Fearless Leader
(may His Name be forever praised!)
like a wise farmer has planted
many fields full of ears

In the particles of dust
from the sandstorms
He is also present; if we would breathe
we must do so very carefully

In those distant clouds
in the heavens above us
hidden cameras record
our every activity

Even the birds on the city rooftops
as well as those in the distant villages
cock beady eyes and fly swiftly
to inform Him of all that we say

Now foreigners come, bearing (they tell us) freedom
— but freedom is only a word we have heard
fluttering like a feather on the lips
of the dying

Coalition Exit Strategy

When the feature movie comes on now in Baghdad
And you and yours are looking at the screen
And a man from management interrupts the screening
To remind you that in case of fire all exits
Are neon-lit and can be clearly seen,

You can't help thinking then, at least in hindsight,
Had someone made a point of this before
You'd have made damned certain when you bought your ticket
That instead of in the *middle* of the action
You'd have got a seat much nearer to the door...

Well, it's far too late to do much now but sit there,
While what seemed like a good night out's become
Problematic: is it your imagination
Or is that *smoke* you smell — and what's that *murmur*
You can hear above the air-conditioner's hum?

You try to focus on the on-screen showdown
(It's the latest Hollywood version of *High Noon*)
But all around you patrons are stampeding,
Torches of ushers flashing in the darkness,
— And tomorrow's come at least a day too soon.

The Coalition of the Uncertain

Iraq, July 2007

Slowly slowly the words begin to move
to accommodate the reality: the dawn landscape
with its anticipated configuration
shining with promise now being seen
in the full light of day
for what it is and was: a prospect
riven with historic hate
booby-trapped with tribal obligations and ambitions
running like trip-wires
through villages towns cities
where the recruiting-offices of mistrust and fear
are always open and death-squads
ride the streets in many suddenly
mutilating forms...
The new heavy-lidded words
blink like tortoises surprised
by the world around them.
                        Step by archaic step
they move, armoured against reproof,
waddling down tracks slippery with yesterday's
Jurassic blood...

'Of Middle-Eastern Appearance...'

'He was, in fact, our third one for the day,
walking along as if he owned the place
– so I gave the lads the usual okay
and let him have one then, fair in the face;
Slugger king-hit him next, Greg sunk the boot,
and Gazza hopped in quickly for his chop,
but there was something weird about this coot:
why would any one of them, ever, want to cop
the lot without a blind word?
                                    Blow by blow,
he stood and took it all...It was as though
he knew what makes us do what any bloke'll
do, whether he's wearing angel's wings or horns...

We celebrated later at this local
beach pub that's called (I think) *The Crown of Thorns.*'

The Banquet-Scene (Abu Ghraib Version)

Can such things be,
And overcome us like a summer's cloud,
Without our special wonder?
Macbeth, Act III, Scene IV

We mini-Macbeths, through the media come
to judgement of a sort in Baghdad daily
— who, it seems, had else been perfect in
pursuit of high ambitions realised
too rarely in this region, must grievously
confront (like the Scottish king) the ghosts of deeds
best hidden from a disapproving world,
and would, had we a choice, like that same king,
dismiss such images speedily...

                             Alas,

the spectres of anonymous Banquos rise
mutely suffering in their nakedness,
and push us from our comfortable seats.
This is most strange: that works intended for
the shame of those marked for harsh questioning
(sly digital shots to be shown to the subjects later
and to soften-up future prisoners) should now,
in this technological market-place the world, be seen
by all and sundry, and any advantage
gained in a military sense henceforth be lost,
while the original shame intended only
for the captive few must, ironically,
be shared now by the honestest of us all...

A Dog in Time

If you're afraid of the wolf, get a dog in time…

Arabic proverb

If world peace were as easy to achieve
as marchers think, bared bellies now declaring
the desirability of making love not war,
why, Priapus would be president-for-life,
all our differences dissolve and Lysistrata score
the Nobel Peace Prize every time!
On to the Acropolis, then! And let's unfurl
Vietnam's mouldy banners once again,
wheel on the obligatory swastikas held in trust
for Uncle Sam, of course, who else, indeed?!
Certainly not that smirking Hitlerite
dodging between his opulent palaces,
in some debauching Nebuchednessar dream…
Street theatre has its place, of course, right here,
as well as in downtown Baghdad, but it hasn't yet
replaced free parliaments and the rule of law.
And isolationism cannot serve us now,
anymore than it did Washington in the thirties
for which the world then paid a tragic price
We like protection, too, of course,
especially when our nightmares come alive
— at other times we like to think ourselves
free, independent, self-reliant souls,
able to make our own way in the dark
and cluttered geopolitical alleyways
and come out shining like Decoré ads…
Would it were always possible! Alas,
we have made enemies of whom we know
too little, ones whose violent vision of peace
does not accord with what the banners say

and who would more cheerfully gut those nubile bellies
than kiss them in an access of desire.

What Television Offers Us Daily

is dark angry swarms of men
mouths and eyes wide with fervour
brandishing Kalashnikovs, holding up
decorative denunciations in Arabic script
and the gravely beautiful faces of women
in burqas, Madonnas at an endless crucifixion,
plus the formal stances and dress of yesterday's
martyrs framing tomorrow's self-immolation
– *and* the airbrushing out by swift editing of
the contextual consequences, thus sparing us
all but the smoking ruins, the blackened skeletons
of cars, buses, occasionally train carriages
and the stunned faces of the still living
– in the wake of such visions we are presented
with the sober reflections of terrorism analysts
(a burgeoning sub-tribe unavailable in the wake of
many earlier slaughterings) the ratiocinations
of the irrational beast in us, ever keen
to incorporate the latest technology into
the age-old driven incomprehensible man, crawling
(as that thirtyish Wittenberg student once said)
between heaven and earth...

Tall Poppies

Poppies bloom in Flanders,
and many a moistened eye
reflects that emblem lovingly
just as in days gone by...
Meanwhile in Helmand province,
Barkundi, Kandahar,
Farah, Badghis, Uruzgan
the poppy is by far
the flower on which a nation
(whose hardihood is famed)
survives, corrupted, bloodied...
and who is to be blamed:
the Taliban? the farmers?
those East and West whose need
creates a ready market,
while stolid soldiers bleed?
7,000 tonnes of opium
in a mad drug-hungry world
are armoured against whatever
technology is hurled
against them by rich foreigners,
however right their cause,
since desperation has its own
inexorable laws.
And now the word is spreading:
those hills and valleys hold
iron, cobalt, copper,
lithium, and gold
– further complicating
factors to punch in
for those prescribing necessary
antidotes to sin.
But deeper than any minerals

(and far less easily shed)
are tribal and clan loyalties
that dominate heart and head...

Going to the Ball

a Totentanz for the 21ˢᵗ century

Will *you* be my partner at the Nuclear Club Ball?
Everyone's going this year...
There'll be free Strontium 90 for one and for all
and if you say Yes I'll be happy to call
and we'll dance the fandango of fear!

There'll be new folks a-plenty from East and from West,
there'll be room for big parties and small:
Kim Jong-il will foot it along with the best,
while in Tehran they're planning another big test
and hoping no fall-out will fall...

The Frogs will be there (if a spot can be found
far away from the lights of Paree),
and the Russkis (and old Uncle Sam, I'll be bound!)
and one or two others who are still underground,
plus Indians and Pakistani.

The Brits will be present and Israel as well
(Arab Emirates are hoping to come),
China, of course, and some rogue-states as well,
although uninvited, will push in pell-mell
(right-of-entry by way of the Bomb...).

Oh, what a fine gathering there'll be, what a bust!
And what a gi-normous great noise!
The neighbours, as usual, will complain as they must,
citing the fighting, the cuss-words, the *dust*
– but boys (like they say) will be *boys*...

And, as sure as God made green apples, then some
will rush out in the car-park and brawl,
while, waltzing, we'll wonder: 'Since business will *hum*
now the earth is awash with pluton-ium
– what on *earth* will we do with it all?!'

Eloi. Eloi...

for Lulu

Observing you in your touchingly dog-like dailiness
as if there were never to be an end to days
of running, shouting, savouring bones held firmly
between hairy fore-paws, pleading out of dark
eyes, snoozing in the sun, or rolling belly-up
with pleasurable grunts on the lounge-room carpet,
it strikes me again how devastatingly alike we are who also
romp (if we're lucky) in the short playtime
of our lives, looking up uncomprehendingly whenever
the final day, hour, moment arrive
– as if to say *My God my dog*
reach out and take from me now
this puzzling all-encompassing darkness
for which (and out of which) we once were born...

A Later Babylon

an intervention ballad
for Bess Nungarrayi Price

By the rivers of grog we sat down and wept,
in the shanties of shame we were broken,
under big-city carpets the promises swept
and all the great statements proved token.
We cried for an end to the fists, the abuse,
and the pollies they all cried: 'We're listening!'
– but the tears of the crocodile matched each excuse
while the tears of the women were still glistening.
This country of ours may be lucky for some,
but, for all the fine words that are spoken,
when will release from captivity come,
when will *these* dead be woken?

Seas

Always I found it, even as a child
in Clayton and, at Christmas, Anglesea
– it breathed forever in my veins (as yours),
caressed its endless sands the same, and later,
at Springvale, married, I found it once again
(or rather, its sands again, easy meat for digging in
and mulching up to grow things as it once
grew underwater gardens, aeons past…).
Now we go to sleep and hear its susurrus
like that of a sleeping child; walking the sand,
note the colour co-ordinates of sea and sky,
or seeing its blue stretch horizon-wide
at a distance, coming down Caloundra Road
and thinking, as so many have,
of Xenophon's expeditionary survivors crying
"Thalassa! Thalassa!", it has the feel of home (those shells
littering the beach could be the ones I played with *then*)
– apartment blocks, and at least one major hoarding, promise
a future like those north and south of here,
since coastal stripping
knows no bounds and while the pelicans
sail imperturbably to and fro and ibis
perched on antennae threaten the boob-tube news, we know
there are seas other than those we frolic litorally on
to which the crows each morning cry black answers
and we, caught as we are between two seas, two childhoods,
for various reasons make the most of it…

Shrapnel

Wherever you look there's Bethlehem and Golgotha;
Crowds deafen many Jerusalems with their cries;
Mary the Mother of God and Mary of Magdala
Are passing along the street before our eyes.

In upper rooms the latest disciples are meeting,
Breaking together both leavened and unleavened bread;
The prodigal son, the rich man (Dives) and Lazarus
Pose questions of mercy and justice for us, instead.

Barabbas is getting the nod, big-talking Peters
Are eating their words on this evening's bulletin;
Samaritans daily surprise us, driven by compassion,
Attend the wounded, pay for them at the inn.

Judas is alive and well and doing business
On many a committee still in many a land,
While Doubting Thomases everywhere must verify
The wound in the side by thrusting in a hand.

* * *

The shrapnel of the Christian gospels is now embedded
In the very flesh of metaphor, there to stay,
Where all the surgeons of scepticism can't remove it,
Though they ply assiduous scalpels night and day.

La Donna Mobile

Now at last her hunger for uninterrupted conversation with
herself
need never end but continue on forever
in the four-wheeled drive, the shopping centre,
the crowded bus,
in the street, on the busy beach
– people, landscapes, other phenomena being merely
part of the rapt audience beholding
this persona presently promenading the boulevarde
of her dreams
smiling behind dark glasses
hand gestures ritualized like the deity Shiva
adjusting her hair's artful waterfalls
in the op-shop window reflection
declaring to the world at large that she (of all people
inhabiting this forlorn planet)
is not alone but rather in possession of
a vibrant life replete with fawning friends
– this segment being simply a captivating sample
like those free offerings of the latest taste sensation
presented to shoppers in supermarket aisles …

Committee Report for the
New Universal Church of Good Intentions

We began our committee-work with a small concession:
    Theories of Creation, after all,
Are open to a wide range of opinions,
    As is the ancient legend of the Fall.

But that oppressive notion of Salvation
    Put too much pressure, surely, on the Soul
(If, by "Soul", you mean that One Indwelling
    Spirit which unites us to the Whole...).

We had, of course, little sympathy with that other
    Mediaeval relict known as Sin;
Being ourselves so thoroughly *non-judgemental,*
    We chucked that nasty concept in the bin!

The Virgin Mary? Well, in these enlightened
    Times that figure's past its use-by date
— A handy subject in Renaissance painting,
    Now liberated from that gender-fate.

The divinity of Christ we thought as prone to
    Much the same uncertainty as the rest
— Better to keep an open mind (like Arian)
    Than put that daunting concept to the test.

By that stage, then, our committee had no problem
    In dealing with such once-contentious terms
As Transubstantiation, which we happily
    Made finally a diet for the worms...

Pope and Priesthood? Once we got our bearings
    As post-conciliar democrats, we saw
That both would have to go, their places taken
    By self-appointed lay-folk at the door.

And (with all due respect) we believe our version
    Of the New Church will suit these times quite well
– A Do-It-Yourself kit with detachable pieces
    To keep you entertained on the road to... Well,

It's not in keeping with contemporary ethics
    To dogmatise on the goals for which we strive
– We may conclude then, that like so many journeys
    There'll be more fun in journeying than to arrive.

George Street

When the family moved to 547 George Street
                                    opposite the gasworks
we had chairs made of car-seats nailed
to wooden boxes, and in the kitchen one of the few
gas-mantels still in use and plaster
falling out of the walls in the passage. When my best friends,
the Simpsons, called I never invited them in,
envying their home with its Abbotsford late-forties
cosiness and their uncle 'Tosca', an affectionate
family fixture. At Studley Park we named
the various landscapes after our Wild West imaginations
(Thunder Prairie, Eagle Butte, and so on). There, we had
fierce rock-fights with blue-metal where no-one
seemed to get hurt. After we left school the Simpsons played
in the Merri Park Cricket Club team with me (I was
an opening bowler). Of all the places of my childhood
George Street I remember best,
on Saturday going to see Fitzroy play in District Cricket:
Roy Hagger and Ray Harvey red-capped waddling out
to open the Fitzroy innings...

Office-boy

While an office-boy at Weigall & Crowther, Solicitors,
                              in Little Collins Street
I had one of the coolest jobs ever: delivering legal letters
to various offices around the city. It was
cool before the word was invented! You had time
for everything and your status suddenly, well,
above that you ever had around the office where you
collected the lipstick-smeared coffee-cups
of the girls in the typing-pool and copied
Last Will and Testaments by hand in the room below stairs
while the legs of passers-by beyond the window
made you feel pre-lapsarian (as did the odd read of
Cleland's *Fanny: Memoirs of a Woman of Pleasure*
passed on to me by the young file-clerk-secretary
in the office next door – the book being a lugubrious trophy
from divorce-court proceedings).
                              It was all too good
to last; at year's-end the junior partner
called me in and, since I "didn't seem to be
                              getting anywhere,"
offered me the choice of a week's pay
or a week's notice. A week's pay suited me fine.
So I left in time for Christmas.

Reading John Morrison

I'll never leave the Left, however much
I palm them off or curse them, they're in touch
by ways and means that have to do with order
and how things ought to be, beyond the border...

Reading Morrison again, I still recall
seeing him at Realist Writers meetings; if the Fall
has literary counterparts those sad, few
times I attended bring that world in view
and he, some twenty years older than me,
I still remember very favourably...
At one meeting there I read some stuff
that got a savaging (and fair enough,
it *was* too Dylan Thomas-ish, I know
even though its treatment then was quite a blow).

Reading Morrison again, I wonder what
became of the young bloke (a sawmill-hand, like me) who got
me to go to the meetings in the first place when
my reading of Koestler, Silone, Orwell, had by then
disabused me of any radical socialist stance
– but I'm still grateful, Chris, for whatever chance
threw us together in that timber-yard,
where the work was risky and bracingly hard
and mistrust of workers placed us in full view
in doorless dunnies.
                              Morrison's true
tales of the wharfies world still speak to me
of whatever endures of solidarity.

Players and Workers

a Public Works Department memory

There were five of us in the gang:
Joey McGrath, the ganger, wiry and tough,
with the saturnine looks and manner of a
natural-born knee-capper; Normie Brown, his faceless
Mafia-style lieutenant; Frank, a labourer pure and simple
with two young kids; Ronnie, the unbright target
of every mean and regular bit of horse-play
– and me for whom a job was still a job
with a room to pay for, food to eat... Every morning
Alan, the young truck-driver picked us up and we'd sit
in the asphalt-stinking back of the truck...
This went on for years. It was
a recognizably fascist grouping, complete with
porky little overseer, (Musssolini in gumboots)
inspecting the progress of each job, and Joey
promising to put in a good word for us
if we kept our noses clean, which really meant
suck up to him, laugh at his jokes
and be forever quietly fearful.

                              The talk
at smoke-ons was of women, times of the month, etc.,
spurred on by any younger women passing
– the usual stuff.

                    Inevitably,
I fell out with Joey, squaring up to him
in the back of the truck one morning (usually
he rode in the cabin with the driver)
– from that time on I knew
I'd cop every shitty job that Joey and his mate
could think of (I was only a worker never a player). So I left.
And never once regretted it; the midday sweat,

the muscle-ache, the ruthlessness,
the way they played the game left a taste that stayed
long after the bitter fruit was thrown away.

Social Anthropology I

for Ken, Peter, Dennis, and Stephany
on my first setting my own poetry as a text for study
after 40 years of teaching

I can hardly believe I'm actually doing all this
– Teaching my Collected Works on a long-term basis
Is as odd as turning one's cheek for a dragon to kiss
In the presence of so many weekly belovéd faces…

I'm taking it all too seriously, I suspect,
(Gathering around me now both study-guide and full-length book,
As if in desperate defence against some exotic sect)
– I'm embarrassed already, hardly knowing where to look

To avoid their various gazes; in this hall
Of mirrors, of course, I'm learning what it *is* I do
(Or have done) and, believe it or not, it's all
Enlightening… I can see, for a start, what you

And others (in interpreting the wandering spoor
Marking the path I've trundled along through the wood)
Have in the end, despite my mixing of metaphor,
Done me and my sense of self some permanent good.

I've never been much of a one for looking up close
At what both morning and evening mirrors reveal,
So, now that I have to, while reigning in the verbose
Temptation to let it all hang out, I find it's a real

Eye-opener, as they say, to learn that, besides
Leaving an errant trail of footprints behind,
There are certain patterns of thought not even my dithering hides,
And behold, now in this clearing sits clearly what *could be* a mind!

* * *

But then, this isn't just a matter of me and those mentors,
However clearly they've shown me to myself
– No, there are forty students also involved now:
As easily reconcile Ghibelline and Guelph!

For years now in my own house they've frequently 'read' me
Through that personal prism home-context can provide,
With domestic furred and hairy members eager to greet them
And the melodious burble of magpies just outside!

Thus, I couldn't possibly enter on literary discussions
With any of the customary Eleusinian airs
A tutor may have, whose impersonal campus background
Enables him to entertain angels unawares,

For all of *these* angels many of *these* poems have contexts
Which only home-based ease and kidding supply,
But now I come freighted with such personal chit-chat
Blurring the texts for all but the strictest eye...

However, thinking it over, perhaps as a compensation,
Such personal addenda at times scrawled on a page
May at least prove of advantage in removing
Any likelihood that I'll be mistaken for a sage...

Stuff Happens

for Ray

> *Like those they call collateral damage, I*
> > *Was helped to leave the system and retire.*
> *Of course I wasn't killed. I didn't die.*
> > *I was just taken out by friendly fire.*
>
> Ray Kelley, 'Quietus'

Your great ballade with its infinitely
memorable refrain has answered, at least for me,
a most troubling question of theology

and one about which always much
debate has centred: Is God losing touch
or is the complexity of the cosmic battle-field now such

that these things simply *happen*, even in a world
where the flag of God's omnipotence is unfurled
somewhere every morning, whether dewy-pearled

or otherwise, so that unintended consequences flow
from what, as far as human HQ know,
is just a simple routine sentry-go?

And while human agency should take the blame
for much that happens in His holy name,
there is, in the fate of many, just the same

no better explanation for the dire
fate that infantry suffer on the wire,
or while sleeping fitfully in some foxhole, that if higher

responsibility is to be attributed then the cause
(as happens in the very best of wars)
comes under the heading of 'Immutable laws',

so that for *homo sapiens*, as for all
of God's embattled creatures, answering the call
of their multifoliate natures, where we fall

is simply the collateral damage of our lot
(except in *this* world, whether we like it or not,
the end result is: *everyone* gets shot).

This Side of Botswana

When we'd go to visit him, he'd recognize us
      but what he'd recognise we were never very sure of
and when he'd talk to his wife we'd become
      increasingly uncertain which of his several past wives
he was thinking of (if it wasn't his present one)
      and which of them he thought he was talking to right now
— the Nows continually shifting and/or coalescing, of course,
      like those past jobs he'd had, here or in Botswana,
and which he believed he still had. He was always very
      passionate about his feelings, as if he was still
in control of them.
                    Meanwhile, this side of Botswana,
we tried to make conversation and be cheerful,
      but what he made of it all we never really knew.

He would like to go home, naturally, and several times
      he escaped from the special ward (once by entering the code
for the locked door, twice by climbing a tree in the grounds
      and getting over the wall). When he *did* get back home
we'd have to trick him into returning by such stratagems
      as professing a keen interest in the new 21-inch TV
he had in his room...
                 Whatever we did, whatever we said,
we still felt guilty and began to watch ourselves more carefully
      for tell-tale signs, do our daily crosswords more religiously,
like traitors who have been pardoned
      by some special act of royal clemency
— at least, for the time being.

Surprise, surprise

for Liz

There was this woman I noticed at this reception
chatting to my step-daughter, Lara, and it seemed to me
(since she was handsome, in a green outfit, shapely as can be)
that I immediately thought: Now *there* is someone
with whom I could pass the time *agreeably* ...

Imagine my surprise and especial pleasure
when, approaching a little closer, I could see
that that attractive woman there was you, dear,
(as, of course, I should have known immediately!).

No longer confused myopically now by distance,
I can see how right I was, then, just the same,
and congratulated myself straightway on my persistence
– plus any other qualities you can name.

The Blazon

Checking old video-tapes for the least embarrassing one,
I came on a garden scene from Cumming Street
where we lived for thirty years and there, in the long chicken run,
were a Rhode Island Red hen and a bantam rooster:
the one, comfortable as a middle-aged mum in sleek brown velvet,
the other, in his shining plumes ablaze with glory...

For days afterwards (and even now) their memory
and that of all the others over those years
processed before me, immortal birds
we never ever destined for the table
but loved for their natural dignity and pride,
pleased to think of them in the evening
retiring like royalty to capacious roosts
in the tall hen-house,
preserving always their hieratic order
— just as Mandela (like that earlier Nelson,
a prince among his people) walked the prison-yard
at his own incomitable pace
despite the fretful harassment of his guards,
in the long darkness dreaming of the day.

Father to Son

at Christmas

"Take my advice: skip entertainment centres
– the big stars will be out to fill the sky,
you wouldn't get a look-in, son, believe me,
it's not the time or place, don't ask me why
– it's just, well, for a start, it's *mega* business,
not your kind of show; very soon you'll be
a refugee from a holocaust like so many
in this (or any other) century...

Well, alright, if you must be part of the action,
let it be elsewhere, some forsaken slum,
or a shelter for the homeless that I know of
– you'll find a home there, till your Kingdom's come."

Remembering Bill

for Thelma

I used to see him carefully picking up
personally every single fallen leaf
in his longish driveway.

Tall, thin, amiable always,
I think he was already stooping towards the ground
when we first moved here.

His invariable greeting to me was
(in a returned digger's well-wishing tone)
"All the best, Bruce!"

Towards the end
I would only hear him singing softly to himself
beyond the fences.

Some people can be garrulous neighbours
for a life-time
and you still hardly know them.

Bill was the other kind.

Creaturing

for Lulu and Prue

This dog and this cat
weave their lives within our own
– the one having learnt to lay
her guilt on us with dark eyes
whose whites are the ultimate beseechment
– the other with her gaze
blandly absent as a lunar landscape,
when her sinuous balletic style
isn't twining us into acquiescence:
we have by now been thoroughly integrated
into their mutual strangeness,
(as they into ours)
– the one with her staccato language
straight from Sirius
– the other lyrically illustrating
the weightlessness on the moon...

All Aboard for Lethe!

for Stephany Steggall

The story of my life is mostly gaps
– with, here and there, a 'maybe' or 'perhaps'.
When I consider other lives I've read,
I think it can be well and truly said:
compared to them I haven't lived at all
(a thing of shreds and patches you'd best call
this interminable stammer of regret
when prompted to remember), 'I forget'
is the constant sorry burden of my song
which has gone on, it seems, for far too long
– how much I enjoy those other writers who
when asked to summarize, can put two
-and-two together and thus make
an equation for their blithe biographer's sake!

Oh, if only I had known, when life began
that out of such details is made a man
– why, then, I would have from my natal week
made shorthand signs before I learned to speak,
and, with my alphabetical years at hand
kept notebooks ready for each ampersand
of narrative Life dictated... Now, alas,
when opportunities beckon I must pass
the buck with frowning brow to you to make
what you *will* of very little – so please take
these *un*heroic couplets penned by me
as (what *was* I saying?) an apology...

The La-La-Land Express

There are claims that the Jakarta Australian Embassy bombing was a US/Australian conspiracy to divide the Moslem world.

On the La-la-land Express, you know,
You can book your seat today
– It'll take you wherever you want to go,
However loopy the way!

If you think the moon is pure Gruyère,
And the world is apple-pie,
If you think that billiard-balls grow hair,
If you think Berkshires can fly,

If you reckon that 9/11 was a sham,
Just another conspiracy plot
By that arch-conspirator, Uncle Sam
(And in La-la-land, why not?),

If you claim that JI (if it exists
At all) is nothing else but
A bunch of young philanthropists
(Plus the odd occasional 'nut'),

Then the La-la-land Express will fill
Your every lunatic need,
And whatever you do and whoever you kill
Or leave in the streets to bleed,

Will be *somebody else's fault*, and lies
At the feet of some Western excess
– While you smirk your way to Paradise
On the La-la-land Express!

The Blue Dress

It was the blue dress
that did it I should have
known it was the wrong
one to wear he mightn't have minded
me wearing the red one
but the blue one was wrong
when will I learn what
he wants I should know by now but
I'm a very slow learner
that burnt dinner the favourite shirt
not ironed the time I forgot
to defrost the fridge I don't
blame him really I'd lash out too
if I was him I'm sorry I tell him
and beg him to stop although I know
it's my fault and the blue dress
is what did it this time next time
I'll make sure I put on the red

The Gulf

for Liz

The heart, the eyes take in
what strikes them like a blow:
the loveliness in your smile
— even though they surely know
(if later they should seek
some worthy way to tell
to all the world what then
rang resonant as a bell...).

to touch your hand and say
some dumb words at the time
can no more span the gulf
than even a life-time's rhyme
can embody the flight of a bird
as it sculpts the morning air,
or the silver leap of a fish
poor human speech declare.

But still, like hands that touch,
we lovers murmuring go
to pay our due respects
to that which 'passeth show'.

The Morning

Came in the morning early
with the usual sweet spices
the holy women hoping
somehow the heavy stone
might from their grieving hearts
be rolled away
– there in the sepulchre finding
angelic messengers telling
them that their Lord was risen,
they took up the folded linen
and began with wonder walking
into the light unfolding
of the ever-living day

Many thousand mornings later,
and many saints the wiser,
may we from tombs of selfhood
by similar witnesses' goodness
move into the future
enlivened by its promise,
to praise and work and pray...

This Heron

This heron comes and goes
from our back lawn when
it suits him/her, landing
in a lanky grey way, small
pointy skull eyeing us until
our dog rushes at it (un
-convincingly), whereupon he/she flaps
clumsily to the toolshed roof, to be fed
seafood cocktail or sardines
from the cat's larder in
the garage – I have often seen
a heron standing in the
sludge on the edge of the
artificial waterways, or sometimes
sedately aloft in flight; whether
it is the same one it is impossible
to say at a distance, but this bird
brings the angular exotic present of its
presence into our lives and a beauty
that is partly its whimsical
materialization at times of its own
choosing. It is this illusion of
casualness which most appeals, as if
it were not hunger, but merely
the flip of the sun's coin in a
daily game of two-up and the off-hand
call of the wind that returns it
to us again
         and again
               and again…

The Other Day

The other day I looked down at our dog
bustling away on one of her innumerable errands,
self-absorbed as any creature can be
and I had this momentously obvious thought:
why, she's... she's... like us, really,
with her humble bourgeois concerns (meals,
a car-ride, the odd benevolent pat,
something to bark at), and I thought
how wonderful most creatures are,
how modest their expectations
– and how often they are not met.
And my heart went out to her, then,
and to all those (in a world designed to hone
unsatisfiable hungers) whose nature it still is
to not ask for too much.

The Walkers

And who, watching this smiling and waving couple,
walking hand-in-hand up Pennsylvania Avenue
to their new official residence
cannot but notice their handsome progress flanked
by heavily-coated men in black
and think of the unseen but ever-ready
snipers on rooftops lining the route
—but who (remembering the polished assurance
this president-to-be always carried
like a marshal's baton in his campaign knapsack)
can forget even now,
(with hope in as many colours as Joseph's coat
shimmering before the nation's eyes)
how fear, the shadowy older brother of hope, will continue
to walk the avenues and halls in the days ahead?

The Three Temptations

'First, limestone into loaves? No, even though
it might have been impressive for a while:
a world made hungerless… But, even so,
the welfare hand-out thing was not my style.
Likewise, the Temple trick: to take a leap
from the very top of Sion: a bungee jump
to beat the record! But to keep
bettering that act forever or risk a slump
in the ratings? No, that would be absurd,
given the crazed addiction people find
in spectacles, as such…

                         But then, that *third*
temptation, which the demonic mind
thinks irresistible: the power
to rule the universe and all that's in it…
Who else could have resisted, in that desert hour
of ultimate seduction, where each minute
offered me what every tyrant craves
but cannot have, although he bathe in blood
and bid all men be slaves?
Do you suppose (being also man) no premature bud
of interest at that prospect came to *me*?
Well, think again… This was no parlour game;
temptation, to be real, must really be
exactly that, and *that* is why I came:
to make my life an endless learning curve
for everyone, to embrace the human flame
and, in doing so, teach others *Whom* to serve.'

This New Century

                    Bertolt Brecht

and you, you say, know nothing of this
since it all comes to you in comfortingly distant images
(this new century already proving murderous enough
suicide bombers flying to bits in their rage of martyrdom
taking non-martyrs with them wherever possible
especially women and children
and the drive-by shooters from grandiloquently named organizations
who sometimes fail even to claim their proud responsibility
and the children from remote villages
sold for sex in Bangkok and cheerfully infected
by those preferring virgins
and the AIDS epidemic like a tribal ghost stalking the African nations
and the child-soldiers conscripted into rebel armies
                              of so-called liberation
and those other millions of little ones toiling from dawn to dusk
who never see school or a reasonable wage
and those thousands grateful for grass bread in Northern Afghanistan
and the drug culture shadowing every land like a cloud
– you, *you* look in the nonchalant mirror
of a magazine or the Plato's cave *wayang* of a jumbo-size TV screen
and suppose you know what it's like out there
where the sky is full of holes through which pour streams of fire and
jagged ice
        and soup of any vile description is a luxury
                and a raw potato discovered in a field
                        is something to fight to the death for)

Time-warp

had Jesus taken up the suggestion that He get down from the cross

'Jesus? Once the wounds had healed he went straight back
to being a chippie.
Matthew's taxing the hell out of us again for those damned Romans,
(with a bit on the side for himself, of course...).
And as for Peter, Andrew, James, and John, they're all out there
on the lake somewhere, (even though their catches are pretty small
these days). And good old Luke, why, he's back doctoring again,
though there's often a faraway look in his eyes
when he's making up a free poultice (he was always
specially concerned for the poor, you know...).
Simon the Zealot, not surprisingly, copped it
when the Romans nabbed him with that nasty little knife
he was aiming to use on them in an alley
some dark night... Judas, on the other hand, I'm told
is doing well in his accountancy business in Samaria;
No, I never see Mark nowadays... Once Peter tossed it in,
Mark didn't have any other occupation, but seeing as how he had
a well-to-do Mum and Dad (or so Paul reckons) I'm pretty sure
he's getting by OK. And, as for that other John,
the one they called 'the beloved disciple', they tell me
he never really did get over it, but then, I guess,
none of them did, one way or another...
I've seen a lot of fellows hanging up there
on that God-forsaken hill, but that Jesus,
he was the only one who seemed to have a special reason
for being there (one too big, I suppose,
to be spoken about these days...).
Barabbas, of course, got lumbered shortly afterwards
...(once a thief, always a thief, I say)...
                              As a matter of fact, Barabbas
got his final come-uppance just last Friday.'

Unsolved Mystery in an Upper-Middle-Class Suburb

In this suburb the lawns, large or small, are neatly trimmed
– if not mercilessly manicured
(we rarely know the people but we *do* recognize their lawns).
But we did know Vicki, however. Shortish, blond, happy,
with her little white terrier.
Her dog wanted to be friends with ours, but ours wasn't having any…
Vicki's husband drives a wide-body white ute. Or, at least, he *did*.
In the years we've lived here, we only saw him once.
Then Vicki disappeared (East Timor, Solomon Islands, we found out later).
The ute didn't move, although one day, months ago, the tray held
 a lot of flattened cardboard cartons.
The lawn disintegrated. Weeds took over. Even the new concrete footpath
was being covered in weeds (here,
we look after our footpaths, too).
Months passed. We never saw the dog anymore
or the daily walks Vicki had with it.
We're not ourselves purists about lawns or weeds, incidentally,
But we wondered, just the same.
The ute never moved. The weeds grew taller. Palm fronds fell,
adding to the air of neglect.
Weeks after Vicki returned from overseas, we went over
and offered to mow the lawn, not asking any questions.
Though maybe the offer itself seemed like a question.
Vicki said she'd get someone to come and mow it. Eventually they did.
More weeks passed.
By this time, even the weeds looked neglected. The ute stayed put.
We could imagine it blending into the background in time
like those rusty tin sheds in long-forgotten paddocks.
Vicki wasn't a hippie, making some anti-bourgeoisie statement.
She was Vicki, and we thought something very sad had happened to her.
And there was no-one she could turn to. And that was even worse.
We felt like weeds.

Watching Football on TV

Every so often
the camera shifts
from the on-field striving
to close-ups of the crowd in the outer
(held in a freeze-frame of anguish, fury,
hope, the dawning of delight)
and we can read there all human history:
the demagogue caught in denunciation, fist raised, glaring,
the child bug-eyed and beautiful
before the engulfing surge of events, the mother
rugged against winter's inclemency, calm and attentive,
the young man studying in his blood the physics of power
– before the game returns to the sad wisdom
of the retired stars' commentary,
with Christi Malthouse like the angel of the Crimea
bearing the latest report from the dressing-room
on the dodgy knee of the key utility player
and the critical recurrence of the hamstring...

Acceptance Speech

Firstly I would like to thank all those people who should, really,
be standing up here with me to receive this award
including Adam, of course, oh, and Eve (wish you were here, sweetie)
as well as those talented members of the cave-folk crew
(too numerous to mention personally, unfortunately) *plus*
the Dorset team (Hi, great-great-great grandad!)
and a whole *slew* of Celtic backup boys and
(what am I saying? *girls*, too, of course!)
You've probably heard all this before, but HONESTLY
without your great support this movie
which for the sake of a better word we'll call My Life
would certainly never have been made... it's all been, well...
A TRULY HUMBLING EXPERIENCE,
if you know what I mean
and at this point I just want to say — what's that?
Oh-oh, looks like I'm getting
that old familiar wind-up signal, folks — *isn't it always the way?!*
Look lemme just say in closing
that it's YOU out there
yes all of you beyond the footlights (can't see a damned thing, actually
— are you still there?)
where was I now?
Oh yes it's all of you out there
that have made it all seem worthwhile:
those hours days months years
MILLENNIA EVEN! and besides
knowing what I know now and
having been chosen this year
by the Universal Academy of Emotional Pictures
and Artless Sciences (love you, guys!)
for this prestigious award...
why, I just feel so PROUD...

so… um… HUMBLE… mumble… mumble… mumble…

(Vast unending inaudible applause)

Lulu

in memoriam, 1995-2009

Your joys became our joys: the imminence
of the daily walk a jiggling excitement
(so many trees to visit, so many lamp-posts!),
the adrenalin rush when neighbourhood dogs
set up their small-dog yapping, the sighting of others
(whether big or small) enough to set your cock-of-the-walk bravado
on display, like Thurber's fabled Scotty who knew too much
a model followed throughout your life, and like most dogs
avid for car-rides, even being known to hide
under the seats in hope of exotic longer trips, the very
tinkle of keys enough to set you running to the garage...
All cats except ours prowl easier now you're gone, but birds
were never really affrighted by your watch-dog's gruff
'Clear off!', usually only intended to impress
us with your 'On the job, boss' assurance when we appeared...
Your large dark eyes still follow us, ever alert, your happy
peg-toothed grin will remain, as will the trees, the beaches
you got used to: routines are often our back-doors to love,
and those we'll also miss in much of the house, like the lounge
whose curtains you nosed aside, enabling you then
to observe the passing parade, a premonitory Glaswegian growl
marking the passing of some old enemy.
Hearing your dream-barking still
in our daylight hours, how can we now *ever*
come to an end of all that we'll miss in missing you?

The Ancients vs Moderns Cricket Match

Skittling Johnson early gave us hope
– those end-stopped couplets could have really been
a major problem... pairing up with Pope,
Sam scoring boundaries like a grave machine,
we'd have been well and truly up the creek
without a poetical paddle, but Bill Blake's
deceptively simple action with that "tweak"
(as Max would call it) gave the lads the shakes,
then Wordsworth's slower ball he calls "the flipper"
(which goes straight through) sent both their bails a-flying.
When Byron, with a few words from the skipper,
came on at the southern end, there's no denying
we knew we had the buggers on the run;
Chaucer went down the pitch in a sprightly dance
and skied a lusty drive, while poor Jack Donne
(full of conceit, as usual) took one chance
too many with a yorker, and the rot
set in right there: Milton popped up a sitter
to Auden at mid-off, Spenser hooked a hot
delivery from Yeats (still feeling bitter
over the Irish question); from then on
– seeing we had the hard runs on the board
their tail-enders (Waller, Dryden, Vaughan)
while not quite bunnies, hardly could have scored
the necessary deficit... 'What's the hurry?!'
yelled someone from the stands
(he had a bush-hat and big beefy hands,
I think, I'm pretty sure it was – Les Murray).

The Stillness

This particular day the wind had dropped:
the trees no longer thrashing in some turbulent dream,
no birds were inscribing on the sky's grey slate
lessons from their necessary primer, the hoarse breathing
of cars was no longer heard, and the green indifferent prose
of the lawn lay like an impenetrable sub-text
between bricks and concrete borders;
everywhere there was a stillness you could hear
and I happened to think: Why, this is *it*, this is the stillness
that comes to us all at times as a premonition
of what lies beyond; it is like the silent guest
at a wedding or funeral who says nothing
and yet is the most eloquent person there
– so for a moment I heard the speech which lives immortally
in the spaces between words, the stillness
awaiting us and all creation,
the patient rocks and the stars

Memorabilia

Blu-Tacked on our garage wall in the name of love
along with grandchildren's art-work
are newspaper photographs of General Monash,
Claus von Stauffenberg, Aung San Suu Kyi,
a NT magistrate in her legal gown fishing,
and a large action shot of Michael Voss as
captain of the Brisbane Lions with a pencilled
Biblical inscription from Daniel 6:24 after a
grand final victory, plus Raffaella Torresan's
drawings from her book, *Literary Animals*
– and a happy photograph of the little boy
in the TV ad who is learning about the origin
of the Great Wall of China from his
well-meaning dad who is obviously
making it all up as he goes along...

Eventide

'Too often, it seems, they do not understand
why we resist (against all reasoning)
that other world which lies so near at hand:
a room with one of the family, the *sensible* thing,
or a Sunset Retirement Centre, replete with friends,
medical staff, social activities, bus-trips, all
the many comfortable ways in which our ends
(and *theirs*, of course) can be accomplished by the small
surrender of living *here*, where home says what we *are*,
lit, as it may be, by the evening star...

So small a sacrifice (you'd think!) and yet
so large and threatening a one for us,
who have so many losses to regret
when we're so aware we're near the terminus.

We sadly shake our heads: from where we live
can they not see that this or that *new* move
could be, *would* be so definitive,
and that although they come to offer with love
an alternative life, so much that's gone
now calls to us to honour that lost past
which made us what we are, and later on
will, like a new-found lover, hold us fast?

Those other futures which they put before us
can never tempt us and are bound to fail,
even though they plead in caring, sharing chorus
– gently but firmly (or with tooth and nail)
we must forego them to that final day
when whatever we have left is taken away.'

Oh, by the way...

for Liz

'We'll just have a light meal'.
you said, and I thought, *Why, yes,*
the possibilities are (practically)
endless:

the morning meal which is brought in
before dawn by the vague and distant sun
– one of the most delicious, an *apéritif*
and one

to prepare our palates for the later
things on the menu, so let's start
(not with those extravagant art-
gallery things *à la carte*)

but breakfast deftly served up by a round-
faced waiter whose beam
-ing *bonhomie's* implied in each
gleam

-ing facet of table-ware laid out in this posh
cafe, *The World*, but then, like a Johnny-come-
lately you're completely struck
dumb

uncertain what cutlery of sense to
take up or in what or
-der to use them (when it's no good doing a quick check
of your neighbour)

And there's lunch already on the way
just when you feel
bloated already from having
so much still

of the day to partake of that you know
already long before dark
you'll be fearful that indeed you may
cark

out at the table embarrassing thereby
whoever's still present, sending them into a tizz,
especially the one whose *bright*
idea this one originally was/*is*...

www.ingramcontent.com/pod-product-compliance
Lightning Source LLC
Chambersburg PA
CBHW030854090426
42737CB00009B/1228